ANGELS

Dear Joan
Happy Christmas!
Love Andi

© 1994 Day Dream Publishing, Inc., Indianapolis, IN 46278
Printed by Shepard Poorman Comm. Corp., Indianapolis, IN 46268
Printed in the United States of America

ISBN 1-57081-771-5
First Edition 1994

Front Cover Photo: Scala/Art Resource, NY

PHOTO CREDITS: Alinari/Art Resource, NY: pages 47; **Alinari/SEAT/Art Resource, NY:** page 51; **Cameraphoto/Art Resource, NY:** page 45; **Giraudon/Art Resource, NY:** pages 17, 37; **Erich Lessing/Art Resource, NY:** pages 5, 29, 35, 39, 53; **Scala/Art Resource, NY:** pages 7, 9, 11, 13, 21, 23, 25, 27, 31, 33, 41, 43, 49; **SuperStock:** pages 15, 19, 55

Has your life been touched by an angel? Some may think that the phenomenon of angel miracles, real-life stories and inspirational works has only been prevalent in recent years. Others agree that angels only appeared in "Bible times", and have not been seen, felt or heard of since.

The truth is that angels have always been there as guardians and a source of comfort; sent as messengers throughout time. The inspiration that they provide can be experienced in *Angels,* a tremendous collection of Renaissance period art. Seekers and sophisticates alike will delight in these beautiful works that are brought together to create a small slice of heaven. A sampling of writings from poets, philosophers, and writers the world over who have found inspiration in these celestial beings is also included for your enjoyment.

It is our hope that these exquisite works of art will fill you with the sense of joy and wonder that must have truly inspired the original artists.

T CAME UPON A MIDNIGHT CLEAR,

THAT GLORIOUS SONG OF OLD

FROM ANGELS BENDING NEAR THE EARTH

TO TOUCH THEIR HARPS OF GOLD.

Raphael. The two angels (detail of the Sistine Madonna). Gemaeldegalerie, Staatliche Kunstsammlungen, Dresden, Germany.

HE ANGELS ALL WERE SINGING OUT OF TUNE,
AND HOARSE WITH HAVING LITTLE ELSE TO DO,
EXCEPTING TO WIND UP THE SUN AND MOON,
OR CURB A RUNAWAY YOUNG STAR OR TWO.

—*Lord Byron*

Fra Angelico. Detail of music-making angel with organ from the altarpiece of the flax-workers. Museo di San Marco, Florence, Italy.

RIDE STILL IS AIMING AT THE BLESS'D ABODES,

MEN WOULD BE ANGELS, ANGELS WOULD BE GODS.

ASPIRING TO BE GOD IF ANGELS FELL,

ASPIRING TO BE ANGELS MEN REBEL.

—Alexander Pope

Filippino Lippi. *The Three Archangels and Tobias* (detail). Galleria Sabauda, Turin, Italy.

ND YET, AS ANGELS IN SOME BRIGHTER DREAMS

CALL TO THE SOUL WHEN MAN DOTH SLEEP,

SO SOME STRANGE THOUGHT TRANSCEND OUR WONTED THEMES,

AND INTO GLORY PEEP.

—*Henry Vaughan*

Rosso Fiorentino. Madonna and Saints (detail). Uffizi, Florence, Italy.

I BELIEVE WE ARE FREE, WITHIN LIMITS, AND YET THERE IS AN UNSEEN HAND, A GUIDING ANGEL, THAT SOMEHOW, LIKE A SUBMERGED PROPELLER, DRIVES US ON.

—*Rabindranath Tagore*

Raphael. An angel. Pinacoteca Civica, Brescia, Italy.

EVERY VISIBLE THING IN THIS WORLD IS PUT IN THE CHARGE OF AN ANGEL.

—*St. Augustine*

Andrea Mantegna. Putti holding tablet (detail from the *Camera Degli Sposi*). Palazzo Ducale, Mantua, Italy.

STONE WALLS DO NOT A PRISON MAKE

NOR IRON BARS A CAGE;

MINDS INNOCENT AND QUIET TAKE

THAT FOR AN HERMITAGE;

IF I HAVE FREEDOM IN MY LOVE,

AND IN MY SOUL AM FREE;

ANGELS ALONE, THAT SOAR ABOVE,

ENJOY SUCH LIBERTY.

—*Richard Lovelace*

Fra Angelico. Musical angels, detail from *Coronation of the Virgin.* Louvre, Paris.

OR FOOLS RUSH IN WHERE ANGELS FEAR TO TREAD.

—Alexander Pope

Master of Avignon. *The Guardian Angel.*

OW CRACKS A NOBLE HEART. GOOD-NIGHT, SWEET PRINCE,
AND FLIGHTS OF ANGELS SING THEE TO THY REST!

—*William Shakespeare,* Hamlet

Rosso Fiorentino. Musical Angel. Uffizi, Florence, Italy.

Y GOD HATH SENT HIS ANGEL, AND HATH SHUT THE LION'S MOUTHS,

THAT THEY HAVE NOT HURT ME.

—Daniel 6:22

Francesco Botticini. *Three Archangels and Tobias.* Uffizi, Florence, Italy.

UT MEN MUST KNOW, THAT IN THIS THEATRE OF MAN'S LIFE
IT IS RESERVED ONLY FOR GOD AND ANGELS TO BE LOOKERS ON.

—Francis Bacon

Melozzo da Forli. Music-making angel (violin). Pinacoteca, Vatican Museums, Vatican State.

T THE ROUND EARTH'S IMAGINED CORNERS BLOW

YOUR TRUMPETS, ANGELS . . .

—*John Donne,* Holy Sonnets

Sebastiano Mainardi. Nativity. Pinacoteca, Vatican Museums, Vatican State.

NGELS ARE BRIGHT STILL, THOUGH THE BRIGHTEST FELL.

—*William Shakespeare,* Macbeth

Leonardo da Vinci. *The Annunciation.* Detail of the angel. 1618. Uffizi, Florence, Italy.

T IS IN RUGGED CRISES, IN UNWEARABLE ENDURANCE,

AND IN AIMS WHICH PUT SYMPATHY OUT OF THE QUESTION,

THAT THE ANGEL IS SHOWN.

—*Ralph Waldo Emerson*

Fra Angelico. Detail from the *Pala dei Linaioli*: angel playing cymbals. San Marco, Florence, Italy.

THE FEATHER, WHENCE THE PEN
WAS SHAPED THAT TRACED THE LIVES OF THESE GOOD MEN,
DROPPED FROM AN ANGEL'S WING.

—*William Wordsworth,* Walton's Book of Lives

Filippino Lippi. The Three Archangels and Tobias (detail). Galleria Sabauda, Turin, Italy.

UR ACTS OUR ANGELS ARE, OR GOOD OR ILL,
OUR FATAL SHADOWS THAT WALK BY US STILL.

—John Fletcher

Peter Paul Rubens. *Annunciation.* 1609. Oil on canvas, 224 x 200 cm. Kunsthistorisches Museum, Vienna, Austria.

OR A GOOD ANGEL WILL GO WITH HIM,

HIS JOURNEY WILL BE SUCCESSFUL, AND

HE WILL COME HOME SAFE AND SOUND.

—*Tob. 5:21*

Girolamo Treviso. *Hagar and Ishmael* (detail). Musee des Beaux-Arts, Rouen, France.

NGELS AND MINISTERS OF GRACE DEFEND US.

—*William Shakespeare,* Hamlet

Filippino Lippi. Madonna and Child with angels (detail). Louvre, Paris, France.

EAR ALL YE ANGELS, PROGENY OF LIGHT,
THRONES, DOMINATIONS, PRINCEDOMS, VIRTUES, POWERS.

—John Milton

Hans Memling. *Madonna and Child in the Rose Garden* (detail). Alte Pinakothek, Munich, Germany.

EVERYTHING WE CALL A TRIAL, A SORROW OR A DUTY;
BELIEVE ME, THAT ANGEL'S HAND IS THERE.

—Fra Giovanni

Fra Angelico. *Annunciation* (detail). Prado, Madrid, Spain.

OW WALK THE ANGELS ON THE WALLS OF HEAVEN,
As sentinels to warn th' immortal souls,
To entertain divine Zenocrate.

—Christopher Marlowe

Andrea di Bartolo. *Coronation of the Virgin* (detail). Ca' d'Oro, Venice, Italy.

EARN, TOO, HOW GOD'S OWN ANGELS KEEP
YOUR WAYS BY DAY, YOUR DREAMS ASLEEP.

—Norreys Jephson O'Connor

Andrea del Sarto. *Annunciation* (detail). Galleria Palatina, Palazzo Pitti, Florence, Italy.

ND ALL THE ANGELS STOOD ROUND ABOUT THE THRONE,
AND ABOUT THE ELDERS AND THE FOUR BEASTS,
AND FELL BEFORE THE THRONE ON THEIR FACES,
AND WORSHIPED GOD.

—Revelation 7:11

Melozzo da Forli. Music-making angel. Pinacoteca, Vatican Museums, Vatican State.

ER ANGEL'S FACE

AS THE GREAT EYE OF HEAVEN SHINED BRIGHT

AND MADE A SUNSHINE IN THE SHADY PLACE.

—*Edmund Spenser,* The Faerie Queen

Giovanni del Ponte. *The Annunciation*, detail of Angel. Abbey of Santa Maria, Rignano sull'Arno (Rosano, FI), Italy.

ILLIONS OF SPIRITUAL CREATURES WALK THE EARTH
UNSEEN, BOTH WHEN WE WAKE AND WHEN WE SLEEP.

—*John Milton,* Paradise Lost

Sandro Botticelli. Four Angels. Detail from the *Madonna of the Magnificat*. Uffizi, Florence, Italy.

TWICE OR THRICE HAD I LOVED THEE,
BEFORE I KNEW THY FACE OR NAME.
SO IN A VOICE, SO IN A SHAPELESS FLAME,
ANGELS AFFECT US OFT, AND WORSHIPED BE.

—John Donne

Pietro Perugino. *The Virgin and Child* (detail). National Gallery, London, England.